Layers

of

Rusty Broadspear

**An epic tour through the mysterious
mind of a multi-sided poet**

ISBN: 978-1-9162980-0-2

First Published 2020. First edition.

Copyright © 2020

For Max and Kahlia

The ones who will one day be obliged to read this book.

CONTENTS

Carousel

The carousel spins and rolls, the cars are a blur,
Accelerating even faster, fuelled by screams and laughter.
An odorous soup of burning oil, candy floss, hot dogs,
Perspiration, perfume, and filled babies' nappies,
Bites into the air – boiling with excitement.
Drizzling rain, seasoned with many wet eyes,
Flying spittle and sprays from a thousand Coke cans.

Bass filled music old and new – fairground music,
Invades all the senses. Soundwaves streaming,
Teeming with throngs, laughing, screaming,
Joking, fighting, yelling, blaspheming, enjoying.
Coloured lights merge and kiss the swirling mist.
Lasers powerfully penetrate a darkening sky.
Toddlers in pushchairs with red, sticky cheeks,
Strain at straps wanting to run into the night, or join in.

Steel superstructures and ramshackle side-stalls
Surround the carousel like Lords and simple peasants.
Invisible vibrant veins feed this breathing site.
They focus on the carousel,
That hums and whirls, faster than an egg whisk.
A loose dog snuffles an empty carton.

A baby reaches into the rain, in vain,
Mother's head is turned toward the carousel,
As are others. They hear a foreign wrenching noise,
Momentarily witnessing, severing, slicing, slashing,
As the ride leaves its pivot
And two thirds of its occupants
Are thrown to Hell.

Clouded Mind

Grey garnished with garlic,
Still, stale with impurity,
Surrounding, enclosing,
Looming over, enfolding,
So still,
And yet mighty,
Drab and untidy,
Yet proud and pompous,
Lacking security,
Unmoving,
Crowded, but lonely,
Packed tight
But not tightly,
Oh move, stubborn mass,
Disperse thee!!
Dreaded anxiety, dam of doubts.
For I love you
And am told from somewhere very deep,
That you love me.

Hit the Street

Amidst the smell of car fumes
Of city sweat
And expensive perfumes,
Amidst the cacophonic screech of traffic
Liberally seasoned with sirens,
Of men digging holes,
Of people noises,
Helicopters and planes,
Amidst the constant jangle
Of my thoughts,
I heard a gunshot.

Close by, I even felt it.
Then, three streets away
Something caught my eye,
It was a body tumbling from a building
I watched it float gracefully
Down the sky.
I didn't hear the sickening thud,
I didn't see the pavement and people
Splattered with guts, bone and blood,
But I felt it.

At the bar that night,
I heard on the news
That three had been killed.
The body scored a direct hit
On a young couple
Shopping for an engagement ring.
I sat at a table and cradled my drink,
My rifle was in the bag beside me,
I took a sip and gave the waitress a wink.

Jasper

The ice-cold Moon was nailed to the sky
Staring down like a blind man's eye.
Invisible visitors scudded through the night,
As Jasper buried bones deep out of sight.

Jasper was a Prince, soon to be King,
He was into magic and all dark things.
Back at the Castle the Queen poured tea,
While Jasper spun a crazy dance of glee.

One-horned beasts barrelled by
Over the horizon and into the sky.
"Where is the King?" thought the Queen with suspicion.
She should have asked Jasper, Jasper the magician.

Blood trickled up through the Castle floors
Finding its way under the heavy old doors,
And the Castle walls began to crack
When she thought she heard the King
But no – Jasper was back!

He exploded into her room all covered in mud
She screamed when she saw he was stomping in blood.
"I've brought some rope," he said, "To see you swing!"
"And by the time you dangle, I will be King!"

The ice-cold Moon was nailed to the sky
Staring down like a blind man's eye.
Invisible visitors scudded through the night,
As Jasper wore the Crown and the bugs began to bite.

Jasper's Corrupt Crusade

Is he sullen, suicidal or depressed?
No – our Jasper is spinningly busy.
His hair dyed orange and anger suppressed,
He's losing his head – or is he?

The dragon couldn't help but smirk
As he spied upon his Kingly jerk,
For he was piercing his nose with a golden pin,
Groaning and moaning as he forced it in.

Cat and dog skins (fresh but fine) were his attire.
He glanced at the dragon as if to enquire,
"What do you think, am I cunningly cool?"
The dragon was hungry and stifled a drool.

After all this hassle, he left the castle
And strode off with a strident gait.
Behind was the dragon, pulling a wagon
Full of treasure and quite a weight.

A sight to see, this comely pair
Huffing and puffing in the chill morning air.
And Jasper's plan, which was artfully laid
Was to find a new land – a noble crusade.

And as the cloak of nightfall whispered down
Jasper stopped and stared, observing a distant town.
"Well, lookee there, Hotlips – now it's time for repose."
And they snored as they slept – until the Sun rose.

Spider's-Eye View of Eric the Writer

In the background, Four Seasons, Vivaldi.
The monitor eerily lights the room.
From my perspective, his face was well lit,
Heavily contoured, studious, at times sad.

He was smoking heavily and drinking malt.
Occasionally his hands clasped before him,
Elbows on the desk, he rested his head,
Staring at the screen, where his dreams had once been.

He was at peace but in thoughtful turmoil
As ideas boiled. He was gently giving birth,
With such care, tenderness and compassion,
To a structure of words
That would make the world cry or laugh,
Or at least stop, think, and believe in hope.

A one-sided smile, a groan, gut laughter,
A tear, a yeehaa, an inward doleful sob,
Emotions ran riot to the mood of Vivaldi.

While he was working, his world was sleeping.

Sporadically he would go outside
Lie down on wet earth and silently ask the stars.
No answers but inspiration aplenty,
Then he would rush back in
And fingers danced the keyboard Swan Lake,
For seconds, maybe minutes…
Then head on hands… he strived.

By the way, my name is Gemses,
I am a female spider perched atop his monitor,
And I monitor this man most nights.

Sometimes he touches me
As if afraid he may hurt me,
He does it to let me know he's aware.
A mindful man, with such deep resources,
A kindful man, not lonely. He has social skills,
With an assignment to which he is comatose.

When awakened…
Now Bond themes are playing,
Shirley Bassey slips him into gear
And fingers tap the dance of the thirties.

As this man swigs another malt,
Gemses says that this man is in love with life,
He embraces it full fold,
Loving everyone without exception.
Gemses says, take care of this man
For he his troubled.
I love this man so much…

It's Not My Party

As an outsider looking in.
The party's in full swing,
Jeremy the surveyor has taken the top of his head off,
People look in and see nothing.
Part of Alice's brain has died,
She's on her seventh gin.
She's groping Andrew
Asking when the party will begin.
Andrew the bank clerk
Falls back on to the music machine,
The music stops,
Alice throws up,
Then she turns green.
Jenny the hostess
Ignores the mess,
Restarts the music
And straightens her dress.
She's holding the party
'Cos her husband's dead,
And left her with money
And a half-empty bed.
Across the room,
She eyes up Mike,
He's got a Porche
And a BMW motorbike.
Martin and Lewis are sharing a chair
Lewis loves Martin
But Martin doesn't care,
He's in love with himself
And his yellow dyed hair.
Mike spots Jenny
Heading his way.

Alice swallows her eighth,
And starts to sway.
Mike turns around
And heads for the door
Thought it was out but it was the bedroom.
Jenny pushes him through, on to the floor.
The music goes soft
The lights dip dim
The general atmosphere
Starts to swim.
Some people get close,
Some further apart.
Then some of them leave,
Having fallen in love.
I took my smile of irony home.

Sugar-Coated Pear Drops

Like sugar-coated pear drops,
The notes scattered from the harp.
As, under the silken Moon
We danced alone
On the patio.
The backdrop of evergreens
Breathed gently
As if in rhythm
To the cascading strings.
We were close as we swayed
Merging hearts, minds and cells.
Hands moved independently
Lightly brushing
Touching
Resting.
Lovers in scarlet flames,
Burning and swaying
Screaming passion but gentle
And warm.
As sugar-coated pear drops
Floated to the ground
All around us
In harmonious accord.

The Fairy Queen

I'm greying round the temples,
I don't feel a young man anymore,
But I dominate the scene and I'm everybody's Queen
Yes, I'm the Fairy Queen that all young bucks adore.
God save me, God save your Fairy Queen.

God save *the* Queen

Young men treat me with the respect I deserve,
Any single one of them I would welcome as my King.
But I keep my distance, as they stand in awe and observe
Then, in unison, they all begin to sing.

God save *the* Queen.

I've seen straight men bend,
When in the spotlight of my eye.
I've seen faces filled with wonderment and admiration.
Yes, I'm *the* Fairy Queen, on that you can rely,
Let God save your Queen from temptation.

God save *the* Queen.

Thoughtful, kind and gentle
Are the words that describe me best.
A divine-like figure in the company of males.
With campness and these qualities I am blessed,
And immaculately dressed in top hat and tails.

God save your Fairy Queen, God save *the* Queen.

Jackie Chan's Party

The room was rapidly darkening, and filling
With a turmoil of emotions.
Jackie Chan was a murderous bitch,
Mixing drinks, poisonous lotions.
Red talons darted from bottle to glass.
Looking so busy, in black velvet and lace
That swept side to side so graciously.
Life in her body and death in her face.
Her guests whom she'd invited
Were flickering, insubstantial fantasies.
No more, no less than room fillers.
Surroundings of the material kind – were his.
He was the man who had taken her life
And twisted it for two miserable years.
Now she'd taken his, with malice and venom,
And wanted none of these souvenirs.
The bow of the cello favoured the bass,
Broodingly amplifying the sombre mood.
Jackie Chan's heart was heavy with hate
For this necessary - unwelcome interlude.
Shadows and movement and murmurings,
Oh, to scream into the perfumed air.
When all these festering wounds were gone,
Her life was mapped out elsewhere.
She smiled as she handed out drinks,
Wanted to puke over the hands that snatched.
Content in her heart, that they wouldn't depart,
It was more of a case of – despatched.

The Tweaze – Part One

The bowl of sugar, stood in the centre of the table,
The Tweaze slid surreptitiously down into the sweetness.
Hidden, apart from the tip of one micro-thin antennae,
It lay still with the slyest of discreetness.

The dining room was empty, until little Pollyanna entered.
She stood with chin on table, sensing the tempting fruit,
Lemons, limes, oranges, raspberries, apples, baby bananas,
Pulling on her ringlets, she thought – *Bananas look cute.*

Her tiny hands peeled and plopped a cute fruit into a dish,
Craving sugar, but even on tippy-toes, it was out of reach.
She wasn't aware, as she climbed on to a chair
Of a near silent, but sibilant, sputtering screech.

There was no spoon, so she dug in with her fingers,
She sprinkled a little but then wanted more.
She didn't usually misbehave and thought she was brave,
But what she got, was not what she'd bargained for.

In her hand was a creature with a mouth but no face,
Two legs, antennae, round body and a pincer like claw.
She had a feeling it was weird, as it lay still in her hand,
Although she'd never felt anything like it before.

The Tweaze – Part Two

Outside, clouds slid by the sliver of silvery moon,
The garden barbecue was filled with drink laced fun,
But in the spectral shadows, the Tweaze were swarming.
For the Tweaze, the fun, had only just begun.

Simultaneously, two Tweaze leapt – with pincers, hung on
To Pollyanna's Mother's eyes, whose mouth howled a cry
Of terror and fright. The party silenced, all gaped in horror,
As the Tweaze gushed forth in plentiful supply.

Within minutes the party was ended in sightless panic,
Pollyanna's Mother and close friend fell on the barbecue,
And they were writhing and twisting and leisurely roasting.
The Tweaze went to the house, where Pollyanna played
With something new.

Hundreds of Tweaze lay still on the dining room table,
They were silent, they were full, relaxed and resigned.
They'd had their fill of fresh tear-filled eyes.

Pollyanna was safe, for she was totally blind.

Rainbows and Flowers

And everything grand,
Warm April showers
On the greenest of land.
There isn't a time
Or even a place,
Where I haven't wandered
Or been face to face
With a vision of love,
So happy and sad,
With Angels above
So good and so bad.

Tree tops and tear drops,
Heaven and Earth,
Blackbird singing…
My love's given birth
To an illusion of wonder,
And a dream of a dream
With lightning and thunder,
And the moon…clotted cream.
She comes and she goes,
The air is left still.
A deep empty void,
With damp morning chill.

Fairgrounds and people,
Perfect peace and noise.
Silhouetted church steeple
And the shout of little boys.

I'm alone, alone
But not for very long…
She vowed, she promised,
I heard it in a song,
I heard it in the breeze,
Finely filtered through the trees.
I saw it within her photograph….
Come back, love...come back please!

Starry Eyes

The warmest heart and starry eyes,
Tropical sun and deep blue skies.
Together we live, together we love
In lands apart and the land above.
Love clouds rolling in our direction,
Leaving once more a bright blue section
For us to walk to hand in hand,
A kiss is a promise, in that far away land.
Stars for neighbours, planets for friends,
A clear, cool breath from an Angel sends
My love to you and yours to me
We fall asleep contentedly.
Dancing alone in a lifelong dream,
To a tune on a heartstring, our own love theme.
Champagne for two, smile from the heart,
Bonded as one, impossible to part.
She awoke to a kiss I longed to give,
Her arms around me we longed to live
Together forever…forever means life,
Darling, my loved one, please be my wife?
A dream, yes a dream, a lifetime it seems,
So far away, my dream of dreams.
If only my love life wasn't unfair,
If I wasn't here and you weren't there
We'd walk up the aisle, to the sound of the choir,
Our hearts would be lifted higher and higher,
Our parents singing, a baby cries……..
I love you…. I love you….my starry eyes.

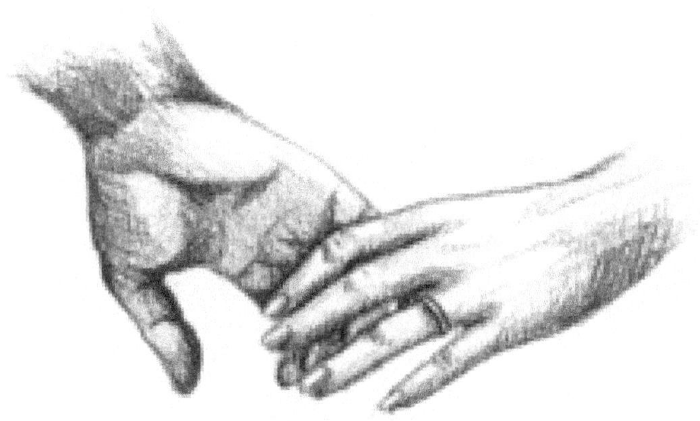

Exit the Avenue of Remembrance

Like life, love lazily turned a corner,
When my attention was distracted,
It could have grown stronger
Instead it became weak.

The baby cried
I picked him up, held him close,
We cried together.

Apart from a tired old chair
The room was bare,
I whispered to the chair,
Asked for a second chance.

The baby slept, my eyes dried,
We stepped into the street
And walked
To the Avenue of Remembrance.

We didn't stop at our house
Her house? Their house?
I didn't see the bricked-up memories
Of her and me
And baby makes three.

We were warm in the afternoon Sun,
He stirred in my arms
And gave a baby giggle,
I smiled,
And wondered for how many others
This day, this hour, this second
Their lives have just begun.

First Moment

Rainbow flavours detonate,
Stars explode in the brain,
Knees knock in aftershocks,
Life rocks
First love, true love
Uncorking grinning champagne.

Multihued visions drift
Between two pairs of eyes.
Whispered secrets enclosed
Life flows
First kiss, such bliss
Unravelling up to the skies.

Monochrome world surrounds
This sphere of shining fire.
Spinning, silent, hushed prose
Life glows
First touch is too much
Embrace to places higher.

Shampoo smells, close-up sighs
One voice.
Probing souls deep inside
Life's slide
First time, so sublime,
Remember the touch and rejoice.

I Ran My Fingers Across Her Name

I have been the Vicar of this parish,
For more than three decades.
I was happily married,
For more than four decades.

I ran my fingers across her name.
So deeply engraved on stone, in brain,
In heart.
Dead leaves danced
In the midst of rain lashed bluster.
The ancient vestry door slammed shut.
A murder of ragged crows
Scattered from the old yew,
Squawking shadows
Like my thoughts,
Flying, nowhere to land,
Thrown aside by random wind –
Flotsam.
Clods of mud freshly dug,
Offering bitter-sweet scent.
Worms oozing out and
Slipping in.
Clods stuck to my boots,
Stuck to my knees.
Dark thoughts, wild dark trees.
Petals and pine needles flung
From forlorn, pitiful dying bouquets.
I was alone in the churchyard,
With other people but
No other human life –
Ironic, uninvited thoughts.

Whispered prayers, ancient and new
Rode the stormy air,
And powerful prayers,
Conjured by tormented souls,
Endeavouring to say
An unfulfilling final farewell.
Then I would offer wisely words,
Assurance of God's presence,
His love.
Reassurance, support.
Silent hope, unheard comfort.

I ran my fingers across her name.
So deeply engraved on stone, in brain
In heart.
People of my parish –
I beg you to avert your eyes,
As I kiss this stone,
Kneed this cloying earth.
Kneeling alone
Searching for my faith and
Endeavouring to say
An unfulfilling final farewell.

Elsie's Precious Christmas Eve

So many Christmases,
Stretching languidly back,
Through diverse ages.

Elsie prepared drinks,
To the tune of 'Walking In the Air',
Her mind flipped back pages
Of her personal book of life.

Her guests, this Christmas Eve
Were few but precious.

Her sister and brother in law,
All the way from Scotland.

Her son, a fully-fledged doctor,
From Brixton Harbour, Devon,
With her daughter in law, a nurse,
Whom she regarded as her daughter.

So many topics to traverse.

She steadily carried drinks into the room.
Her family were snacking,
Smiling, talking quietly, relaxing.
A real Christmas ambience.
The drinks were gratefully received,
One by one, with a Christmas cheer.

Conversation bounced lightly,
Like puffballs around the room,
Of golden childhood memories,
Of journeys and family adventures.

Singers in the street
Filled the room with a hush of carols.
The fire blazed promise.
Dark sky threatened snow.
Scented window candles. Each one a prayer.

Elsie, so proud of her family, raised her glass,
With a smile.
"May love and peace reign over us."

Christmas Eve stepped lightly back with a curtsey,
To allow in Christmas day.

Elsie began to clear untouched snacks and drinks.
Then switched off the light and closed the door…………

To an ever-empty room.

Although the stairs were dark and cold,
There was warmth and light in her heart.
Outside, snow silently tumbled.
Santa rode high on his sleigh.
And Elsie flew free with the Angels,
As she soundly slept.

May Queen

Harlequin dancers with tambourines,
Wooden sticks, high kicks,
Rehearsed routines,
White 'kerchiefs with feminine flicks.

On cobbled street, under midday heat,
Crowds hustled and bustled around.
Children danced with dainty feet
As the Queen of the May was crowned.

Maypole ribbons waved and weaved
A pattern a rainbow would fade for.
Music crammed air invisibly heaved.
The aroma of the roasts, a definite draw.

Pure sixteen, the Queen on the throne,
Waved shyly at the crowd.
Her life was made, her sequins sewn,
Bashful, yet so proud.

She rode a decorated horse-drawn float.
Behind her, a full parade.
In the shade, a poet with quill quietly wrote
All that he surveyed.

And he wrote words of exquisiteness
About life, beauty, love and the kind.
Stroking expressions with sweet caress
About the compassion of humankind.

The parade clattered by,
Confetti thrown from dusty fanlights.
May Queen and poet eye to eye,
He rose from his stool, then quickly writes…

More words, but of his love of the May Queen.
Then he follows the dancing parade.
Falling over children he hadn't seen
She was pure, sweet as home-made lemonade.

The long-haired poet was also sixteen
Searching humanity, for loveliness.
He'd found it, in misty hues, his own May Queen.
A Queen today but his Princess.

The parade stopped, along with his heart.
She dismounted, fell into his arms.
Music silenced, spit-roasts stopped, crowds fell apart
Cheering at the sight of new love's charms.

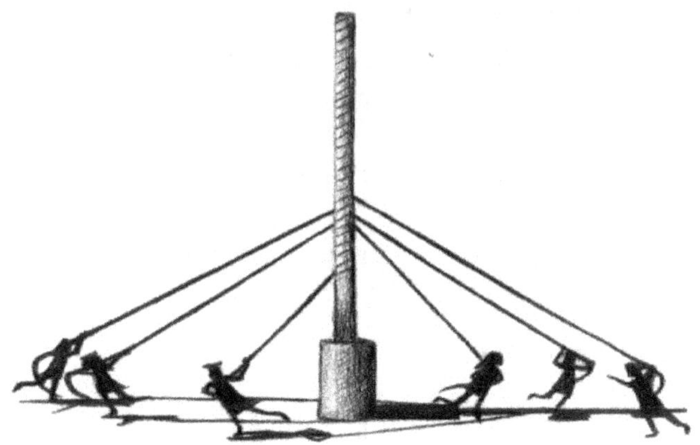

To You Alone

Hey – give the reader and me
Some space, for a twosome.
Okay – that's nice – just us two.
Now – take my emotions
And juice 'em!!

That's right!! Now I'll blend yours.
Put both in the shaker and shake.
Pour two shots of purple blue
Over black ice.
Here's to us and here's yours – take.

Laid back, eh? Feel me feel you.
I cry your laugh, you smile my cry.
You see my dreams – I dream you.
We hug for the ride
And rock sway while we fly.

No such things as lies now,
While I feel you surf my tide.
Your eyes reflect both you and me
And my eyes are windows.
We cannot hide.

Another shot – let's go deeper.
Human race – rush of blood.
Wow!! – Feel that surge of life?
We speak in silence
Screaming – this is good!

Videorama with Dolby Surround
Fast forward – births to nows.
We swim away

To our own cranial caves
Wiping our sweaty brows.

Well – now I know why you read this
And what you truly thought.
And you know why I wrote it
Our knowing is raw intimacy
That we found yet never sought.

My Man and Me – Part One

Tonight's walk was something else!
Boy! The smells!
Also got to meet
The new dog up the street
Scruffy git but very fit
And the way he sniffed me, was rather sweet.
Hope to see him again sometime.

When we got to the meadow
My man slipped my chain.
Well ……… did I run?
It started to rain
I slipped again and again.
Twice I rolled over,
Why, I can't explain
But always in smelly stuff
Like other doggy do-do
Or dead animals and their pong is totally rough.

Sometimes with muddy paws
And slobbering jaws
I'd jump up at my man.
He'd push me away, playfully,
Making me bark sprayfully.
My man would shout
I'd run away, stop, then chase my tail
Until I was dizzy.
Oh! The joy of outside and the freedom trail.

Bit of a downer when we got back,
My woman washed me down with a hose.
Hey! Get that thing off me!
She bared her teeth (her version of happy!)

Don't ruin a good night!
Got my own back – I shook and shook and shook.
That made her jump back,
Always does.

My man and me had a good walk tonight,
I pondered ………………..
As I lay damp, hungry and shivering.
I knew my woman wouldn't feed me,
Not tonight
But that was alright, 'cos she didn't need me,
Not like my man did.
My man and me make a team
Like pebbles in a stream
Like scones and clotted cream
Like scenes within a dream ……….

That was about the point
When I stepped, tail waggingly,
Into my own glorious dream.

My Man and Me – Part Two

My man and me go for car rides
And when my woman stays at home
I sit up front.
If it's a nice day, the windows down
And my head's out
Ears flapping like a canine clown
Willing my man to go faster
And faster, ready for take-off,
Mouth open, tongue lolling.

Wow!! The air hits me with a million
Passing scents.
Too much ecstasy, overload.
Nice overload – hit me with more – I can take it!
Excitement intense
On the open road.
We get into the countryside,
Animals everywhere,
A whole feast in every beast.
Not that I'd kill one.
Wouldn't be fair.

My man yells and points,
Hey! Thanks, my man – I see woods coming up!
Stop the car, I love the woods,
Scents are deep, concentrated.
Noises make me alert
All senses inflated
Mark my territory with many a squirt.
My man doesn't stop
I look back longingly
My ears blow over my eyes
So I don't see much.

Sometimes we stop at the woods
Not always.
Good days and there are better days.
Before we get home I jump in the back
My woman thinks the front is her seat.
We pull into the drive,
Don't want a smack,
So I pretend to be asleep.
Woman comes out – and she knows!
Comes out holding a brush,
Cleans the front seat
Then sprays some slush,
Foul-smelling slush – hurts my nose.

Wherever my man goes,
I always goes,
Don't you knows…

One-Hole Golf Match

Ferdinand Furker is my label.
And golf is my game.
My opponent in this match
Is Mabel – a golfer of little fame.

The hole was the other side of town.
One-hole course, over a mile.
Mabel won the toss at the traffic lights
And teed off with a pleasant smile.

I followed with a slice.
She hit her ball into a taxi bay –
Which, for me, was nice.
Mine rolled into a shop called Safeway.

Mabel dragged the unconscious taxi driver
To one side
And followed up
With a shot that was far too wide.

I sliced again, perfectly plopping the ball
Into a freezer filled with frozen veg.
Mabel was getting cut and bruised
Shooting from a hedge.

Feet firmly planted
On bags of chips and peas
And hitting the ball squarely
Through the shop window with ease.

They insisted on taking the baby out
Before Mabel climbed into the pram.
As her club swung backwards
Mother and baby decided to scram.

My ball rested like an egg in a nest
On top of a kid's Big Mac.
He grudgingly placed it on the ground.
I gave the ball a whack.

The lid of the burger flew with it
So I gave the kid my loose change,
Enough to cover the burger, and he cried
Which I thought was strange.

Such a sweet stroke old Mabel played
Then she rode the pram down the hill,
Overtaking the ball, which was after all,
Quite an unusual thrill.

One good bounce then a ricochet,
I was now atop a six-foot wall.
Precariously balanced I took a swing
And couldn't help but fall.

Leg either side, saved by my crotch,
I gingerly eased myself down.
With balls like grapefruit, and not up to much
I cautiously crept into town.

Mabel was stopping the traffic
Playing a shot as sweet as a nut.
Raising her fist in cute defiance,
Then a car ran over her foot.

Legs wide apart, on the edge of the park,
A nine iron would do me fine.
The ball arced through the air, a perfect shot,
The trophy, (a sky lark), was mine.

Mabel limped to the top of the hill,
Her ball nestled in a rose bed.
She untied her hair, then hit the ball square
Into the back of an old man's head.

Two shots to go, if all goes well,
And maybe I could do it in one.
But I hit the ball and for the life of me
I didn't know where it had gone.

It seemed like an age this futile search
And Mabel was going ahead.
Then the 'Big Mac' kid pointed at the pond,
I thanked him and patted his head.

Up to my waist in water
To my crotch it was welcome relief.
The ball rolled up and over the bank,
Which, surely, was beyond belief.

Setting myself up for an important shot,
Knowing Mabel was near the hole,
I played it with everything thing I'd got,
But the damned thing went out of control.

Went high in the air, hit an eagle,
Came down hard and bounced off a rock,
Hitting Mabel, hard and fast in her gaping mouth,
She keeled over and died with the shock.

Releasing the ball from her oral grip,
I decided to putt for the hole,
Twelve easy inches - it surely must drop,
But it stopped on the edge of the bowl.

I took the flag, broke it in half
And kicked my ball away,
Then in the hole, I saw Mabel's ball,
So she'd won…………

I cried
And called it a day.

Eyes of Deep Sighs

It was so intense, a still snapshot moment,
I was drawn into her eyes.
Happily wading in and very soon drowning.
Strong undercurrents from all directions
Pulling, pushing, stretching,
Painlessly dissecting,
Into inner sanctums,
Private, assertive.
Feeling capture with freedom,
Ecstasy with torment, swirling, churning.
As we stood under the orange halo
Of a streetlamp,
Bedraggled in light rain.
Moments ago, my proposal accepted.
My palms held her cold wet cheeks,
Her nose was red, her eyes were wide,
No need for more words.
Eye contact beyond all boundaries,
All else was lost,
To whoever wanted all else.
It was time to explore.
Dizzily spinning,
Calling her name over and over, distant replies
In these eyes of deep sighs.
Wanting no more
But to remain and explore.
Slowly I surfaced
To subtle changing colours,
To saltwater and rain
And release from all pain.
So lovingly close tenderly tight,
The kiss carried us through this memorable night.

Eyes of Deep Sighs - Morning

Spellbound.
The rain ceased, the Sun awoke,
No one spoke.
There was a chill, we were warm
With our opening dawn.
On a bench in the park,
Her head rested under my chin.
Was she sleeping?
Fleeting morning fragrances
Born on fresh dampness,
With breakfast birdsong.
Lonely souls walking dogs
Silhouetted against virginal skies.
But above all else, I was with her
And my memories,
Of those eyes of deep sighs.
I kissed her hair,
Ran a finger under her chin,
She looked up, sleepily smiling,
Our lips softly brushed,
As Autumn leaves
Floated down one by one.
The park slowly came to life,
A warden gave us a knowing smile
As he passed us by.
Hugging tight, not wanting to let go,
Pure ecstasy and bliss,
When those eyes of deep sighs demanded
A final feather of a kiss.

Expensive Boots

One of those Summer sunsets
You know, like a snapshot
A flashbulb instant.
Beautiful yet depressing.
For it's a moment in time
Not noticed by most
And will surely be lost.

The slag lay naked in the dirt.
An evil voice told me to leave her.

The pain had long since gone,
Except for that damned bright
Silver lining hurting her eyes.
No time to make good
And no time for goodbyes.
His face was a study,
A dark Angel,
He was quite beautiful.

She was broken.
A suitable package for our Maker.
I leaned down close
And forgave her.
Ignoring the voice of evil
I erased her
With the heel of my boot.

A wad of dirty gum stuck to the sole.
He really should clean
Those expensive boots.

The sunset came and went
And the following day
Was fine.
The traffic was heavy
So I stopped for refreshment.

I felt sorry for the waitress,
She was a slut.
I asked her out.
She admired my boots.
They weren't made for walkin'.

Road to Ruin

A bush shadow shot into the road, I swerved.
I was unnerved, the night before I hadn't slept.
Jumpy, twitchy and sad, the road curved.
In a black mood playing with blue devils, I kept
My line on the bend. Over halfway there,
With a whispered prayer. Shuffled the radio dial,
Bebop, ragtime, blues, I'll take rock 'n' roll.
Ventilate the volume to each decrepit mile.
Sing with the boys, drunk on noise, gain control.
Trouble is, I was carrying a trio of uninvited hikers
- Gloomy, Despondent and Downbeat.

I coughed a sob and that made them excited.
Rock of Elvis stopped. Now crying in the chapel.
Gluttonously gorging the road but fuel was low.
Wiping palm sweat on pants in a morbid trance,
Streetlamps danced by like running chorus girls.
Glance at the clock, keep this speed, I have a chance.
Was hope next to me? I patted an invisible knee,
Friend don't go. I drove up to the hospital door.
The surgeon met me, immediately upset me,
I felt my head hit the hard, tiled floor.

My kids were all right.
Good news dressed in dark disguise?
Their Mummy now shone
As a star in the skies.

Locked Doors, Locked People, Locked Minds

I find myself motionless, inactive, blank,
Turn, turn, turn around, nowhere to go.
Unshakeably grounded, locked out
Washed up and on the rocks – *Hello!!*

Anyone there? Can someone let me in?
All around me, is inert, inactive, numb,
Locked doors, locked people, locked minds
What have I, or what have they, become?

A sense of fatalism, circumstances dictated.
Tears swell, I let them fall
They turn to ice, shatter at my feet.
Another locked door, in another brick wall.

Tendrils of my mind reach out far and away,
In search of a mind that has something to say.
But they reach locked people,
With locked minds, I stand alone in dismay.

I feel dejected and totally rejected,
Like an old wedding bouquet lying by the road.
My whole being, on the verge of collapse
As my spirit erodes, as my thoughts explode.

Locked doors, locked people, locked minds.
Behind one of the doors, there maybe someone like me.
Oh to see that face and enjoy spiritual embrace,
To make my escape and forever fly free.

To Be a Kool Kid In the Sixties

I am a student of the sixties
I am seventeen, male and going on old.
Beatles, Beach Boys and Stones covers
Keep me warm in a life that is cold.
I live in the sixties.
Not for me Eminem and DJ Who,
But it's not just music you know.
I've learned…
It was cool to be free,
It was cool to do drugs,
Be a hippie
Indulge in Flower Power
Be a student of Pop Art
Psychedelic, maaan!
Listen to the spirit of the house brick
As it splits apart
To Mr Tambourine Man
Or Strawberry Fields Forever.
Beach battles,
Mods and Rockers.
Take a flower, maaan,
Make love not war.
Pop concerts, naked dancing,
Sport with streakers.
Yoko, Andy Warhol,
Vietnam
Kennedy's life and death.

Let's not forget
The mystery and magic and romance
That was abruptly taken away
And replaced with awe and wonder
When those blokes

Leapt with heavy boots
Across the Moon.
Elvis.
Joss sticks, mini skirts,
Objections to war.
The cold war was freezing
But better than killing.
What made the Sixties different
As I see it as a student in the new millennium,
It was a momentary oasis in time
When the young g-g-generation ruled.
I am only seventeen, going on old
And they still try to p-p-put me d-d-down
But now they succeed.
I really don't want or need today
At seventeen
It's the sixties I need.

Young Love's Expectations

The one I adored,
Was, to me, my only possession,
Someone to care for,
Someone to love, and to love me,
Someone to cherish,
And to fill my heart with pride,
And hid me, in her heart,
When they laughed.
Who accepted my decisions,
And would live with me happily,
Willing to struggle through our hardships,
And to dismiss my mistakes.
Someone with the instinct
Only mothers have….
That is, to love, wholeheartedly, without display.

A glance from her,
And I would feel,
Vibrations,
Sensations,
And I would grope into the air for more,
Enter into her heart,
And feel the warmth and love,
Her guaranteed protection.
Her loving affection
Would fill my heart
With the burning desire
To love her.

She was mine
To carry through this world
And the next.
We were as one.

And the bond between us
Could only be broken by death.
And she died
On the eve of our wedding night.
No one to carry her over the threshold.
And now……
I have died also.

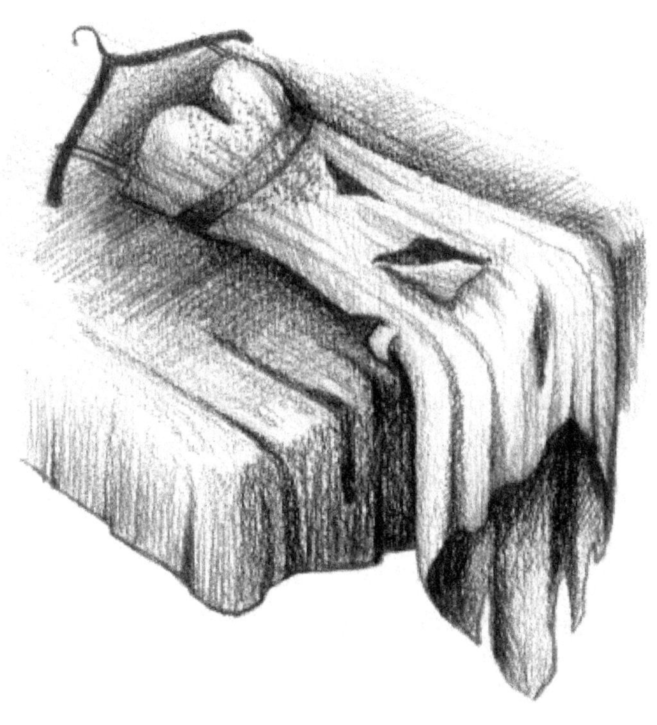

Goodbye Grandma

Young Jimmy's mind was focused on the Game Boy.
He sat at the foot of his Grandma's bed,
He knew she was dying.
Sunlight streamed through the ground-floor window,
It was difficult to see the screen,
He knew his Mum was crying.

She was bending low over Grandma,
Whispering and stroking her hair.
Earlier she'd asked him to leave the room,
But he said he was OK.
She needed him there, he knew that,
At least until the doctor arrived.
Grandma's pallid face was sunken,
Her hair had blown away.

Jimmy heard her cough up phlegm,
He looked up and saw her smile.
She mouthed, 'My Jimmy.'
Jimmy needed the toilet but went back to his game.
Mum puffed up the pillows, Grandma groaned,
A bird on the window sill
Chirped and pruned,
A car pulled up, the bird fluttered and fell, it was lame.

Jimmy ran to the front door,
Doctor Tom looked grim, he let him in.
Tom headed for the back room where Grandma lay.
Jimmy remained outside the room,
The door was ajar, so he listened.
"My love," "Injection," "Too late," "I love you,"
"Oh Mum,"
"Pray".

Jimmy slouched away to the foot of the stairs,
Sat and sobbed.
A cloud momentarily blotted the Sun from every window.
Minutes stretched unnoticed.
Mum had her arm around him.
She needed comforting,
Her soft, distraught sobs made him feel painfully low.

He heard the word "arrangements,"
As the doctor was closing the door behind him.
Grandma's house shivered,
He and Mum rocked gently, holding tight.
As they locked the door and left the house,
The Sun appeared so bright,
Jimmy bent down, picked up the bird, stroked it,
It seemed so right.

Lay-Zee-Boy Days

Billy, John, Speck, Steeleye and Me

It was real Lay-Zee-Boy Days,
Just rocking on the grass and the weeds.
And Speck who lay beside me
Dropped his butt into a turn-up of John's tweeds.
John didn't notice the joke until he smelled the smoke,
And I knew it would provoke…
Trouble.
'Cos John liked his suit,
(He thought he looked cute)
So he spoke:
What the heck, Speck!
(Raising his foot to stomp Speck's head.)
Smokin'll be the death o' you.
Speck rolled over and told Steeleye to tell 'Smart' John
He was taboo,
And John's time on Steeleye's land was through.
But Steeleye's mind had begun to flex,
Side-steppin' bounced cheques,
And his next crate of Beck's.

Billy gave me the eye,
On this laziest of Lay-Zee-Boy Days.
Billy was the youngest, simplest and prettiest,
He liked readin' and carnation bouquets.
Did his eye imply that I should reply?
So I said, *Billy get me a beer and bring it here.*
First he froze,
Then his colour rose.
I watched him disappear.

Steeleye said *Rusty, why'd you treat him like that?*
He ain't queer, he's just that way.
I licked my teeth like I'm prone to do, 'cos it sure was a
Lay-Zee-Boy Day.

John brushed himself down and spruced himself up.
Billy told him how nice he looked.
Steeleye spat a wad of Beck's on to a honeybee –
It was so hot it nearly cooked.

Eleanor pulled up in a smokin' pick-up truck,
Took some groceries indoors.
Say, Eleanor! Steeleye shouted.
You git us some beers whilst doin' your chores?
Treatin' us like dirt, she ignored us,
But we thought we heard a scream.
Billy brought my beer – he didn't get a *Thank you,*
No way! Too extreme.

So Speck, I said, *You and John goin' for some beers?*
Before he spoke, I knew he would say,
We're in the same can as you, Steeleye and Billy,
We're broke.

So while the tumbleweed rolled and the church bells tolled,
Us five were all in praise
Of bus delays and the golden haze of blistering middays.
Yip, these sure were Lay-Zee-Boy Days.

Hugs In Lonesome Street

Unavoidably, inevitably bearing
A lifetimes accumulation,
Of weights and fates.
I stand stooped,
In history's lengthening shadows.
As the day unhurriedly dies,
I shiver to the cries
From unseen gallows.

Hug me warm.

For deep within the caverns of my soul,
One by one,
Endless strings of bulbs,
Dim, flicker, silently explode.
Thoughts expire
Or wander aimlessly
As senses are slowed.
Trembling, I grasp my twilight's briar.

Hug me silent.

For words will not heal,
Or steal the creeping hand of fate.
The chatter of birds
Provide a welcome echo within,
Masking noiseless words.
Insanity in my grip,
To devour, if I should so wish.
Then slip into a concluding trip.

Hug me, rock me.

For childhood awaits
And maybe these weights
Will evaporate.
I thank the world,
With undisguised gratitude,
For my humble moments
Treading its boards.
My very self applauds.

Hug me close.

For as footsteps
Reverberate in lonesome street,
I whisper goodbyes to tribulations.
My part, as yet, incomplete.
For I have something to say
With remnants of hopes and expectations.

I hug you with love.

Retirement Bay

Sugary pink clouds drawn together
Not far from where the bloody Sun
Decided to rest her head.

On the ocean she laid a path
Of dancing jewels.
A sailboat slickly skimmed the scene.

Albatross, by 10cc, in headphones,
Accompanied my lonely vigil,
Amongst the rocks of Retirement Bay.

Wanting no more harsh bright days,
I laid down my sticks and rested,
Reliving life.

The nurses stole my solitude.
I showed them my private heaven.
They smiled, gathered my sticks,
And guided me home.

Neon

Throughout the body of life
There is one thin vein
Of happiness.
Accept it
Grasp it
Don't let go.
Nearly invisible
Greasy on the catch
Always on the peripheral
So get your fingers round it
Hold on
Don't let it slip away.
Pull it from the abyss
Hold it
Lie with it
Succour mutual comfort,
Let the breath of life
Wash you,
Accept circumstance
Go and flow
Down the dirty, drizzly gutter
To the world of neon.

Jasper's Journey

Jasper was a man, an ordinary man
He also happened to be a King
Of a country with no folk
And that's not a joke.
He needed people more than anything.

So..........
While sipping from a flagon
He hitched his Dragon to a waggon
And set off for lands anew.
Driving through the years
Crying many lonely tears
He really was worn out, through and through.

Then..........

In the distance he espied
A golden city and that implied
Lots of folk for him to rule.
So he whipped his beast to make him run,
And combed his hair – gosh, this was fun,
He really did feel cool.

First ....

He met a maiden, oh so cute
Pulled on the reins and stopped his brute.
Where goest thou, my maiden fair
And what thou think of mine orange hair?
She smiled and bowed her head of gold
You must be the King of whom we've been told
Would come one day from lands elsewhere.

Subsequently ....

The news of Jasper's arrival spread
Instead of anger, there was instead
Joyfulness, elation, willingness to cheer
Let's drink, let's party, our Jasper's here!
As Jasper rode in and his Dragon died.
Everyone cheered, no one cried.
Jasper found his castle,
Jasper – the Pioneer.

Release

Everyone dancing the streets
Including kids in old clothes
With new eyes
Piercing the drizzle
To distant skies.
New-born laughter,
Friendship with strangers,
Grinning faces, diverse races.
Barriers fell,
No dangers.
Locked doors opened.
Faith filled faces,
Appeared
Disappeared
Reappeared, to meet
People dancing the street.
Television news staff
Shot through doors
Into the street,
To capture the rapture,
Not into camera
But into their lives.
Whirlpools of litter
Whipped frenzies of delight.
Ice-cream cheeks glowed
In spite
Of the newness of night.
Seconds prolonged,
Everyone belonged,
For what it's worth,
Not only in this town,
But all over the Earth.

Passionate pounding on my door,
No choice but to open.
It was my neighbour,
We'd never talked before.
Said there was something to see
I said, not for me.
He dragged me outside
From the cell where I hide.
I fell to my knees
Like so many refugees
Who find haven,
Open arms,
Humanity,
Sanity.
Discarded vanity.
I cried happiness and humility,
At the futility of life,
Contradicting a desirability to live,
To hold, to grasp, to give.
I felt chilled, fulfilled
Bemused, confused.
Nevertheless,
After serving life in a cell,
I found happiness.

Stormforce

Storm clouds stomp across the sky
Battalions of dark soldiers
Dressed in black, on the attack.
Treacle-thick shadows race,
Cling to contours of the ground
Promising menace.
Everything else is motionless,
Waiting, anticipating…
The air is sickly sweet and sour
Charged with magnetic power.
Even bats stay in tonight.
A dagger of light
Streaks high above the clouds.
A momentary x-ray…
Do clouds have veins and bones?
The light display accelerates,
Colours, angles, sheet and fork.
The battalion lets loose its guns
Booming and crashing,
Blinding light flashing.
Clouds slow down,
Take a deep breath and hold it
…………………………then unleash.
Water falls,
Flood gates open
Such wondrous, thunderous display.

Not Your Religion

The deeper the emotion, the more difficult it is to see,
But the actions are felt.
The shallower the emotion,
Then it is readily seen and heard,
But the actions are imperceptible.

Ultimately, I have found my own religion.
I have found the right way,
Which is the wrong way for all others.

I realise now that I stepped on to Planet Turd accidentally,
On my way to a far greater destination.

As I wipe my boots
I bid you all farewell.

Journeys Together Around Forever

Backdrop – a comfortable lounge in a manor house,
Lights dimmed. Frank Sinatra doing it his way.
Sharing a bottle of old wine, we didn't converse.
Our minds rode the road of a long and varied yesterday.

Masses toiled and died. Generations passed by.
Great Wall of China was built, crumbled and fell.
Composers composed. Signatures destined for a future,
Of swing, pop, punk, a future none would want to foretell.

Nations, races, religions fought, moved around the globe.
Species of animal, insect, fauna, arrived with beauty,
Then went.
We observed our ancestors struggle, survive, fail, succeed.
Beauty of the birth of humanity, watching it ferment.

Ambience around us suggested Sinatra was long gone.
Jennifer Rush powered 'The Power of Love.'
Crying with the world many times in the 20th century,
Holding tight to each other, watching from above.

Grandfather time announced a very late hour.
The room blinked flame lashes of fire.
Raising glasses, eyes and souls locked,
We were in love, yet we flew even higher.

Riding time and space. Like minds as one.
Love, light, compassion, powers to heal.
Our passion shone.
We ride the tide, we spin the wheel.

The night John Lennon serenaded us with 'Woman'
Inadvertently taking a flight into the future. I was alone.
The lounge flickers silently, frightening scenes on a screen.
I travel back. Rescue her from what should be unknown.

The boy from 'The House of the Rising Sun' was not me
Born into untold riches. Access to other worlds.
I shouldn't have invited and trained her. Love was enough.
She wanted to share. I was there. Our lives unfurled.

Dating Agency

I read you because I need you
I need to know you, you are unique.
Within touch, I need to read you,
For we are strong, yet we are weak.

I love you – my heart tells me.
Need to meet, to make complete
Parallel love lines ad infinitum
Need to bend, need to meet.

You're a darling,
Please forgive the cheese.
My heart tells me – I love you,
My mind and body agrees.

Yet still I don't know you.
You don't know me.
But I know your mind and what I find
Is beautiful simplicity.

Why

Where does the source of the problem lay?
Inner space or outer space?
I beg you to slap me.
For am I here or over there?
'I am I said' said Neil Diamond, eh?
I take it, we're all the same.
At least Neil and I.
Did I hear a lengthy sigh?
I wonder why.
Am I trapped or am I free?

The problem is with all of you,
It's also with me.
Tell me then, my intellectual friend,
When did it begin?
And where does it finish?
My childhood questions grow stronger,
They certainly don't diminish.
'Every man is an island,' no longer rings true.

Every man is a star,
Shining bright, unapproachable,
Unable to move.
Watching the swing of planets,
Close friends,
But never the twain shall meet.
Communication is the name of the game,
But now it's anonymous,
Only the handshake of an email.
We are all, without exception, serving life.
All we ask is a word with the prison officer,
To ask why.

Nigel and Prunella

But Nigel is such a crashing bore.
Thought he was going to stay the night.
You say you love him Prunella,
Despite him being such a grey fella.
I was delighted when he walked through the door.
Out – that is – on his way home.
Over time, he will cure my insomnia,
Or he will turn me to drink.
What of conversation, Prunella?
Does he fertilise your mind to think
Beyond horizons new?
When you're both alone
Does he glow brighter than dull grey bone?
Tonight he talked of the value of grass
And how hills would slide without it.
I said there would be nowhere to graze my ass.
Did he see the joke? I doubt it.
When he stated that music was overrated,
A jumble of pitches and tones,
An accepted form of noise pollution………...
I suddenly felt deflated, mistily sedated,
Lazily searching for a solution
To silence my inner groans.
As Nigel droned and droned,
I looked at you, Prunella,
As you sat so prim, gazing at him
As if he was made of Aztec gold,
As if his heart was yours to hold.
Well – my dear – Nigel's nice but oh so dim.
He told me quietly, he was a little uptight
And seriously considering
Parting his hair on the right.
I said – go ahead, you have the right shaped head –

Well, thank you Ma'am.
He is sooo polite.
But Prunella, he's so dumb and then some.
He's so dull, a numbskull.

I leave it to you
And if you two wed
I will wish you the best
But with heart-filled dread.

Last Post

When I was ninety-five, life was sweet,

Contemplation.

Thoughts took daily rides
In my magical flying chair.
Blissfully dribbling, a daily treat.

Appreciation.

I was alive, and in the face of a future.

Salvation.

Sometimes took to the mystical beach
Or to the streets,
Everything within reach.

Compensation.

Happy woman helper three times a week.

Aggravation.

Make sure my cushion smells of piss.
Smoke hard on my pipe.
Unhappy woman. Pure bliss.

Domination.

Mystical beach in shades of blue.

Inspiration.

The sound of sea slapping sand,
The Sun rocking to the rhythm.
Oh yes, this was playland.

Meditation.

Streets were happy or full of rage.

Transformation.

I didn't mind, I tuned my mind,
Savouring every moment
And every morsel I could find.

Perspiration.

One-hundred-and-one, under the lights.

Operation.

Old dribble-dick has had his day.
He's filled my hand all these years.
What more can I say?

Castration.

Cockroach

I see exquisite inscrutability
In the face of a cockroach.
In fact – I call him / her
Pokerface.

Under the magnifier
I think he needs to lighten up.
He scuttles for crumbs
Then stands stock still,
Until…

I throw more scraps.
Perhaps he's jaded,
Armour-plated boredom,
Bushed with exploredom,
And furthermoredom,
Probably wants a mate.

Never too late,
So I collected six,
Unsure of their sex.
And sprinkled them
Into Pokerface's glass tank.
Wow did they scamper and fight.

I threw in some food.
Switched off the light.
They are busiest at night.

Bless 'em.

In the morning,
At the edge of the tank,
They waited for me,
Waving their head gear.
Otherwise standing stock still,
Until…

I scattered more bread.
Expressionless their heads lifted,
Watched my bread-filled hand…….
So… Pokerface had told them.
Probably in payment
For a session.

They really do enjoy their food.
An indefinable robotic cuteness,
(You must think I'm mad),
Polished blackness,
With a knackness
For devouring.

OK – they spread disease
But then so do we when we sneeze.
I say we start a crusade
For these misportrayed night crusaders
That continually raid for food.

Hold a magnifier,
Look into the face of a Pokerface
And see exquisite inscrutability.

So cute.

Rescue

Dawn alighted the night train.
Sun blinked off shining shields, armour,
Breastplates and chainmail.
Sun winked off stirrups and bridles.
Twelve patient knights on tolerant white stallion.
An abundance of loyalty, courtesy, prowess.
A readiness to die for the King.

Awaiting final instruction
To rescue the Princess.
Sir Tristam, first in line
For he was betrothed to the fine lady.
A Nobleman appeared
And read from a scroll.
In unison they galloped
Into a virginal sunshiny day.
The Nobleman watched
A winking, blinking Sun
Race toward distant horizon.

Princess Aelita rode with Sir Tristam,
A tight embrace around his waist.
They rode amid stallion pack,
Protection.
The rescue a success,
A combination of numbers and surprise.
As the day once more caught the night rain,
They were close to the King's Court.
The King would pay handsomely
And Sir Tristam and Princess Aelita
Would be proffered a date
For matrimony.

True Urban

84

Give me a canvass and brushes
And let me paint you a picture.
For I am sure you don't understand
My uncomfortable dilemma,
My solitary circumstance.

I will paint a countryside mansion,
Gleaming white, and central
To acres of rolling grounds.
Matchstick people socialise
Under the proudest of Summer skies.

In the distance you will see the hunt,
Listen carefully for the hue and cries.
A horse rears up, throwing its rider.
Waitresses scamper the party
Serving tea and cucumber sandwiches.

The drapes of a ground floor window
Frame his Lord and Ladyship,
Who haughtily survey the party.
Not a hell-raiser but a fund-raiser,
Towards the upkeep of their home.

A group of heirs to fortunes
Share a table. Bottles and glasses
On the grass around them.
Raucous laughter, chastising a waitress,
And yelling an order for more drinks.

Off to one side, young girls in long dresses
Play tag, with boys in shorts and white shirts.
A girl has fallen and is dirty and crying,
A boy grins and pokes fun.
Motley activities under a punishing Sun.

The foreground I have left until last,
For it corrupts this traditional scene.
A prostrate man under cardboard,
Unshaven, unclean, against
A concrete wall that is about to fall.

He is not aware of the scene behind him,
Or of the precarious state of the wall.
Arm raised, he wakens, to the sounds and smells
Of a backstreet that is reborn,
Every day, in the same dismal way.

Give what you will for my picture, sir,
For you will be buying a hundred different stories.
Stories of fortune and stories of fate
Buy now, read my picture, before it's too late.

Gondolier Street

The passengers hung on
Tolerating the tumbling tram
As it hurtled out of control,
Down the steps of Gondolier Street.

I stood frozen
Dropped my daily shopping,
Looking down at spilled milk
And frail feminine silk
Thinking of the day ahead
That was going to be snatched
Despatched.

Within the next few glorious seconds.
Like a delicate shot on the yellow
Rolling to a sure destination on the baize,
I curiously watched the tram
Through the early morning haze.

Gondolier Street, renowned for quiet
Was in for a riot.
I held up my arms as if in surprise
But found no voice
And had no choice.
SLAM, BAM……. WHEW!
That hurt.

But not like I thought it would.
Like a hammer hitting a stake of wood
Inconsequential
But essential to life,
To the plan for Man.

Realisation when I was off my feet
Minced meat,
Unwritten history
One of life's mysteries.

We lay side by side in the park
In love, and made our vows.
But the afore-said memory haunts me
From my youth and it taunts me.
I'll have to think it through
Because if it's true,
Then life's pretty,
Inconsequential,
And I must live, not for the past
But for the nows.

Grin, Boy, Grin

Are these grinning skeletons taking the piss?
Loved ones we've lost or just people we miss.
The evil knowing grin doesn't fit into the scheme
Unearthly and out of tune, not the right theme.

The boy stood at the graveside
Chucking dirt on to his Mother's coffin
As these thoughts of his Mother's future
Started him sobbin'.

As a Priest I'd read this lost boy's mind
Took him to one side, said 'Seek and you will find'
He said, 'Stuff you! Just get my Mum back!'
I declined, I was lost, with thoughts entwined.

I didn't like this boy.

But now I lie in a hospital bed
My life took many twists and turns, but enough said
For now I will soon be dead.
The priest leaning over me, delivering last rites
Was the boy – Oh joy! Oh joy!
'Do you feel like grinnin' Daddy-o
'Cos if you don't, you soon will be.
Now, just before you die, tell me why.'

I watched my body being lowered
Hey – it's no big deal!
And then I looked at the boy's face
Oooooh that was unreal
Then I thought future teeth in future grin
That boy's my MIDNIGHT MEAL!

Water

The paintwork around the doors and windows glistened,
The wallpaper became damp and begun to peel and fall,
I was as calm as ocean waves in the eye of a storm,
I knew the hit and hurt would come with the squall.

The bed was filthy, head was numb, clothes were damp.
The Moon was low, as was I. The dark hurt my eyes.
I was jerky, excitable, agitated, I turned on the lamp.
No food, no drink, only needles and stuff. New supplies.

The ceiling dripped water, I know, I felt it on my skin.
I saw water in my veins as I lay in indoor rain
I knew the hell-bound hit was about to begin
I was going insane, but in no state to complain.

The filthy stinking mattress was now a waterbed
Man, I was rocking descending bad and fast.
This, was not for kids, this was watershed
And believe me, readers, this awareness doesn't last.

It was when I was riding the reaper's cart, I saw water.
Pure, uncontaminated, not good enough to inject,
I was on the slab, raw meat, or queuing for slaughter.
I wasn't steak, chops or minced beef, I was wrecked.

But you see now my students, you innocent young folk,
I'm in a home, I can't move nothing but my head.
I survived, someone phoned, and when I awoke
I was in good hands –
I could be dead in that wet room instead.

Weekend With Grandma

I looked at Grandma's gnarled hands
As she spoke of times long gone.
A finger tapped silently against the chintz
It held a worn wedding band,
Hiding history I would never understand.

I looked up at her wrinkled face,
White wispy hair and mottled head.
Her teeth came loose sometimes.
Her hand clasped mine,
I was frightened, her face leaned in close.
She was a ghost.

She told me a secret. I didn't listen.
The room was dark, with a tick-tock clock.
Her breath was papery thin,
Like her skin.
I loved her but didn't.
Wanted to get away.
Her grip was tight.
She hissed her love for me.
But she didn't kiss me.

I had an urge; wanted to go to bed.
Play cowboys and Indians that were inside my head.
Grandma was saying
Or maybe she was praying
Words I didn't understand.
I wanted away
Wanted to say
Leave me alone –
But love floated in stale air.

The room in almost complete darkness
Apart from softly creeping moonlight.
The budgerigar slept,
An embroidered cover over the cage.
I invited an inner calmness
But displayed an outer rage.
Snatched my hand away,
I didn't want to stay.
Grandma had had her day.

On a Clear Winter Night

On a clear winter night,
Standing alone, atop a heather-clad hillside,
I turn and turn,
And revel at the dance of the stars.
Clean, biting air reddens my face.
Nature presents me with a perfumed bouquet,
As she rests in sleep,
Contemplating another day.
Such simple solitude.
How could something so magnificent,
So utterly breath-taking
Be enhanced even further, deeper?

To share such a moment
Would make for flawless perfection.
A new outlook on wonder, with
Tender, gentle, and warm affection.

Stuff

Kissing, smelling, feeling
Any old stuff and
Hold it close to my heart.
Why do I value the insignificant?
It's not stuff with value.
Why can't I sling it
Dump it
Give it away
To the needy
To the greedy
Sell it or destroy it?
Instead I hold it
Searching for strange vibrations
I find them...
Or I make them up.
Then feel good or bad
Or more than likely – very sad.
A lace cloth to stand things on,
A penknife,
A monogrammed handkerchief,
An ornament from a travelling fair.
A button box, stirring senses
From each and every button.
Spanners smell of grease and flesh.
A scrap of wood, an off-cut
Smell, touch, feel the feel.
An old book
Sniff, feel, embrace the history.
No-one to ask so make it up.
Bring on the tears and then
Lie foetal, feeling lonely and desolate,
Hugging, so tightly, this stuff.

Smile

Bewildered, beaten, four-year-old boy
Sits in a doorway,
And beneath the muck, the facial make-up,
He raises a flicker of a smile.

You see, when the wind plays a tune
That your hair can dance to,
You feel it.
And so did the boy.
The bruising and abusing took a tranquil path,
Then spontaneously he produced a
Flicker of a smile.

Plastic bags hopped and skipped by,
Cigarette ends ran around in circles,
Weeds in the pavement
Rocked back and forth
Attracting his attention.
Momentarily gone
Were feelings
Of apprehension.

He touched his sore arms and legs,
Then studied his hands.
A strange thought occurred to this four-year-old.

One day
Maybe
These will be old man's hands,
And when they are…

Will I be able to feel the wind?
Will my hair dance?
Will it raise me a smile?
Will these hands paint or make music?
Will these hands hold gentleness and love?

Will I make others smile?

His thoughts shivered deep
Into an inner place.
Tears rivered,
Streaking his face.
In a breeze so slight
Hair began to dance
Eyes closed tight
Breathing in a trance

Then

A flicker of a smile.

Close Call

They sat facing each other across the cluttered table.
Tattered files, sad residue from a failed university course.
Sunlight spiked from a foil strip of painkillers,
One tablet remained.
Two empty tea-stained mugs.

They quietly discussed divorce.
Sad faces talked about times and places.

Behind her, a tap dripped
Into a bowl of unfinished washing up.

Unexpectedly he grinned,
When she made mention of their honeymoon,
Five years behind in time,
When hopes and wishes were plans.
How she wished she hadn't sinned.
So obviously still in love,
Yet he couldn't accept her indiscretion.

Three-year-old Anna was with friends.
He knew he would lose her.

The phone played a distant alert,
A code, saying 'I am off the hook', yet
If every woman on Earth was on offer,
Her eyes told him he would choose her.

A piled bowl of mixed fruit,
Drying, wrinkling, attracting fruit flies,
Topped with an orange.

The oven exhaled breaths of ancient happy meals.

Both faces spilled uncontrolled tears.
Fears of loss, fears of future.
Desperate to touch but couldn't. Imprudence heals,
imprudence reveals.

Tina, the terrier, snuggled in her basket under the table,
Pushing her snout further into her rear end.

They were talking quietly, everything was sound.
Like huge spiders, their hands crept closer
One nudged the fruit bowl.
The orange rocked gently, rolled, fell,
Found a path to the floor – so profound…

Because the noise brought their hands together.
Slight touch, you understand.
So powerful.

Anna played with hose pipe and friends on a sunny day.

Time stood still, dark in this kitchen.
Hands grasped, tears turned to floods.
A cloud darkened the kitchen,
Yet love, once again, came out to play.

Bad King Jasper's Back

Bad King Jasper was feeding his family –
To his new dragon,
When a gigantic dragonfly buzzed his head,
So he battered this wire-bird with his cousin's leg,
Until the blessed thing was dead.

"There is no more food," he cried to his dragon,
"I must speak to my peoples and make them hear."
They must work for me until their bones snap,
For I am the King they all revere.

The dragon snorted a tiny blue flame, while outside
The Sun bobbled down behind dark hills.
Jasper prepared, with body piercing and orange hair,
To make a speech – his thrill of thrills.

The unwashed, diseased and interbred
In thousands cheered their benevolent King,
He said he and his dragon were underfed
And the throng then did the weirdest thing.

One by one they fell at his feet
And yelled to Jasper, "We'll be your meat!!"
"Very well," said Jasper and as if on cue,
He picked up a juicy one to make a meat stew.

It's hardly fair to call King Jasper bad,
He's had a long-distance guilt-trip since eating his Dad.
But Jasper reigned happily until whereupon
There were no people left, he'd eaten every one.

Sweet Masquerade

Mid-morning mist drifting,
Sun can't quite break through.
Freshness, newness, overwhelming,
Thoughts and dreams askew.

Reach out when sleep absorbs you,
Fly the fibre optic sky.
Laughter makes the Angels smile
And the Devil's gremlins cry.

Hands of time roll backwards
To journeys never made,
To lovers lost and lovers new.
Such sweet masquerade.

Look at me now, for I am here,
Don't deny me or look away.
I have a chance, a second chance,
Tomorrow is my today.

The Car and the Indian

The Indian Warrior watched
As his son was tied to the stake.
The child didn't watch
As he ran across the road,
No time for the car to brake.

Tears fell from the Warrior's eyes
His son was doing his best.
The driver saw the child too late
To brake. So he drove
Like a man possessed.

His body clenched
At the feel of hot steel,
He saw his Father kneel.
The car kicked the kerb and started to slide
Child and car sure to collide.

The Indian Warrior watched
Scorching steel slice
Through his son's neck.
The street was silent
The car was a wreck.

The Indian Warrior was led away
His son surely an Indian Brave.
The child lay still
In a hospital bed
The driver was prepared for the grave.

The doctors said he should be dead
But they couldn't see into the child's head.
He was pulled back from the line
By a thread so fine
Pulled by an Indian Brave
Who was long, long dead.

The Couch

Don't tell me what my thoughts are
Or I'll grab your poking nose
And tear it from your face
Then I'll chew it up and spit it out
And parcel it in lace.
I've paid for the privilege
Of your rich idle time
Give me the benefit of sanity
Whilst I'm sinking in profit and grime.
Pan pipes make me nervous
So spice me with rhythm or rap,
Show me what's good, understood?
Stop your mamby-pamby crap.
Use the voice you use
When you yell at your wife.
Whispers tell dangerous lies
That cut like a rusty knife.
Next time we'll meet at my place
With the fairies at the bottom of the dell
And you'll lie down with your arse on the grass,
And then you'll have stories to tell.
I counted down from five to one
Speaking softly, he thought I'd gone,
I closed my eyes and let my mind drift
To happier times
With smiles and miles of green grass
Blue seas
Friendship, happiness, life, life, life,
And when the Sun shone.

To Treasure

Pure simpleness and infallibility,
Without blemish.
Faultless impeccability,
A good Mother's love for child.

Hushed, indiscernible, unspoken,
Without pageant.
A union never broken,
An essence from the wild.

Instinctive and mutual attraction,
Without hindrance.
Safe, satisfaction,
Never to be defiled.

For the families that do not hold the key,
To this priceless treasure chest,
Please be happy for the ones that do,
For they are truly blessed.
Another form of love may visit
Unexpectedly, out of the blue,
And if it does, then hold and grasp,
This treasure sent to you.

Jazz Jazz Razzmatazz

Shhhh snickety snick, shdoosh, shdoosh
Supple wrists guiding agile hands,
Painting tempo light, across the skin of the snare.
Behind shades, Mister Sex embraces Mister Sax,
In unison, swaying back and forth, whilst
The rest of the band relax, away from the glare.

Acoustic guitarist silently tunes and glances
Through cloud at the building crowd, as
In one dark corner they instigate a moderate sway.
The little bloke puts out his smoke, downs his beer,
Twizzles his double bass, like son with drunken mother.
The clarinettist, strokes beard, steps in the light, and plays.

A swollen trumpeter saunters on from the side,
Blasting air from stretched lungs and cheeks,
Into and out of a gleaming silver banshee horn.
A signal to the remainder, to play, stomp 'n' move.
The stage is ablaze, hysterical, possessed, as
The crowd rise to their feet and an evening is born.

A big woman, black, bedecked in jewellery 'n' large hair,
With gin bottle in hand, pushed the bar away.
Unwinding a snail's trail of syrupy, recognisable perfume,
The mass made polite way with unheard applause.
Hefted to the stage, all lights swung, centred.
Silent acclaim, under the howl of music, filled the room.

Shhhh snickety snick, shdoosh, shdoosh,
Whispering intro, anticipation, cut glass about to crack.
Glitter claws grasp mike, pianist stands, stretches, sits.
Laughing eyes and organ keyboard teeth contrast.
Cut glass cracks, with her opening crystal note
And the multitude go feral into hyperactive fits.

And later the mood changes, requests thrown in,
Coloured, reddish lights compose hazy proceedings.
Tips the bottle as Mister Sex embraces her fulsome waist,
Slips into song, like squeezing stockings up to thighs.
Phantom couples, slide across the dance floor,
As time stands still for lovers, no urgency and no haste.

The bottle stands empty and the room is sparse, bare,
The cloud thins, chairs scrape the floor, clean air invades.
Band and singer collect payment from behind the bar.
Loading the van on a chilly starlit morning,
The little bloke gives way to all the beers before,
To the background of a twang of a dropped guitar.

Jessica

The wind was punching everything in sight,
Clouds paced impatiently as if migrating,
The Sun peek-a-booed time and time again,
The dog chased his tail, endlessly rotating.

Jessica was five, stood alone in the garden,
With plaits, and bare arms holding, clutching Sue,
The rag doll that she found on the beach ,
When she was little, looking for her shoe.

Uncle Stan, 'orrible man, sent her down here
When he wanted to kiss Mummy. She didn't cry,
Not anymore. Took comfort from Sue, her friend,
Sharing problems that were in plentiful supply.

The gate slapped in rhythm against the post
Jessica and Sue dance-twirled like the old hound,
The bushes, trees, the whole garden rocked'n'rolled,
Then Sue flew through the air, landed hard on the ground.

The mutt got there first and frenziedly shook Sue,
Jessica screamed, *Drop Her!,* but her words flew away,
Followed by woolly bits of doll, to migrate with the clouds.
No-one heard Jessica's sobs that fearful, fateful day.

At the front of the house Uncle Stan, the 'orrible man
Was kissing Mummy goodbye,
Until the wind snatched him from Mummy's arms,
And frisked him and whisked him, up into the sky.

Jessica looked up and watched Uncle Stan fly.

Birds and Men

A pair of crows flew overhead.
Seems like nothing strange,
But it charged me with 'weird',
And replaced my heart,
With a grisly lump of expectant change.

Now two specks, flapping and flopping
Into the distant crimson horizon,
Maybe to return as a two-headed phoenix.
I sat on the bench and beheld
Two suits walk by with ties on.

Upright and stern, they looked killer-mean.
I watched their backs become silhouettes.
Now, seemed like then.
Pairs of birds and pairs of men.
This rear end of booze and cigarettes.

Family, friends and sleep have deserted me.
Tonight, home is this slatted bench.
Men and birds in flight together.
I am the exception, as I embark
On my cruise of vileness and stench.

Missing Days

"Was a Sunny Day," as Paul Simon said,
As I stood atop a grassy hill.

I looked to the North, then I looked to the South,
And a great, big, red-hot ball of shit hit me in the mouth.

I looked to the East, then I looked to the West,
Another great, big, red-hot ball of shit hit me in the chest.

Back to bed
Sleep the day away.
So I did.

As George Harrison said,
"My Sweet Lord."

Voluntary Refugee

The music was quiet with her mood,
She picked at her food.
Alone with her worst fears
And flowing tears.

Preparing to face derision
She'd made her decision.
Her kids would cope.
Or was that false hope?

Husband would cry a few days,
But that would be a phase.
When her bags were packed
And her mind intact.

She'd be on the train,
Never to return again.
It would be totally absurd
To leave a string of written words.

Just go. A voluntary refugee,
Leaving loved ones, to be free.
Her kids would not leave her mind,
So tough to leave them both behind.

To such a selfish deed she was resigned,
As she packed her bags, her mind was blind.
The train sped on, she cried dry tears,
Carrying memories. Sad souvenirs.

Halfway House

A tapestry of medieval scenes
Bordered the otherwise dull room.
Shafts of dusty sunlight
Sliced easily through the gloom.

Mahogany doors hung open
She entered with apprehension.
An ornate chair moved just a tad,
But the tapestry caught her attention.

She pulled the drapes, to see the scenes…
Torment, persecution, torture, rape.
The heavy oak table moved just a tad.
She was shaking, sweating – had to escape.

The hallway cat floated, not strutted
Beneath the tall metronomic clock.
Arched her back and raised her fur
In front of the doors she took stock.

The room wasn't right in bright sunlight.
The walls were spattered with dark.
A lady lay cut, cut bad, mmm – night bites
The cat ran when she heard a bark.

The room lay still, dark and quiet, apart
From the cat licking, snuffling its meal.
The scenes on the tapestry moved just a tad.
Times past, times present and time unreal.

Walking the Blade and Lying With Strangers

Juggling fine china
We walk the blade
Falling, surviving
Always afraid.

Snowflake falls
Silent death.
Young child tastes
His final breath.

Walking the blade
Through shimmering tears,
Tired and worn
Darkness nears.

I love you and
I don't know your name.
No need for goodbyes
Or the hand of blame.

Feeling cool comfort
We lay in the shade.
It's all over now that
We've walked the blade.

And then we lie with strangers…

Spinning Gold

Pastel streaks of yellows and blues
Streamed down through the willow on the street corner.
The still puddles in the gutter absorbed these hues
It felt righteous, and like I was baptising my feet.

Gently swirling the water, the filth was hidden
Under the willow filtered harvest. I forgot it was there.
Sometimes it pays not to remember. Now it is forbidden.
Thoughts are cast away with a silent prayer.

Timewaves ebbed into the night as the lamps blinked on
One by one. No colours now, just an ink blot, a stain.
I stepped out, and found my feet, but still felt incomplete.
Fragments of 'What a Wonderful World' dodged the rain,
Casting shadows of loneliness, into a bleak, deserted street.

I looked at the willow, which by now was truly weeping.
The wedding ring turned time slowly. Spinning gold
Into the ebony patch, which was greedily keeping
Secrets from the world.

I walked to a new life, having buried the old.

Words

These words are tumbling ceaselessly,
Shattering silently before they hit the ground,
Bursting into kaleidoscopic colour,
A myriad of streaks.

I see statements, promises, questions, pledges,
compliments, '*I love you*'s and lies.
The air endowed with colour turns tragically into greys.

These words are served on a china plate,
The edge decorated in blue and gold.
The meat is the very essence of an assurance,
The substance of a lover's pact.

The salad is the flowery language,
Decorating a sworn statement of fidelity.
The potatoes are the filling, the stuffing,
The contents that make up the package in any form.

These words we see on a journey
With the family in the car or alone on the train.
The trees or the streetlights flash by,
Scorning and scoffing, no commitment whatsoever.

The undulating fields and pastures
Present themselves, and then exit gracefully,
Like a promise made which you know to be true,
But at a later date somehow, eludes you.

These words we see in the weather,
An electric storm, a ferocious argument, followed by
A sultry sunny morning when all is warm and safe
And the words are sugary and sweet,
Followed by the fog, silent, serene,
With sticky little whispers laced with panic,
Chased by an ice-cold starlit night
When whispers are shouted and the truth is heard by all.

These words are on the electronic highway,
Inaccurate, improper, not true, no substance.
Click here to win, click here to lose,
Click anywhere for all you'll find is words.
Download the life of Maggie O'Brian,
She's quite a woman and you know we're not lyin',
Send me your number to my email address,
For whatever you want, you know I'll say yes.

These are the words you'll hear every day,
Like *'Thanks very much'* and *'Have a nice day'*.
'The weather's turning cold'
'No, you don't look too old'
'I hope we'll meet again'
'I think that dress suits you'
'Do you think this dress suits me?'
'I'm washing my hair tonight'.

Words that are bright and sparkling, full of feelgood,
Before they fade and take flight.

Korky Strumpledon

Korky Strumpledon wore a crumpled dinner suit,
A tall white pointed hat,
White winkle-pickers,
Extra-large white gloves,
And that was that.

Korky walked the bustling streets,
Fuelled from litter bins and handouts.
Crossed the traffic river-rapids,
Without so much as a look,
Oblivious to the shouts.

Korky always carried a wooden crate,
That once held twenty-four premium beers.
Sometimes, at an intersection, he would stand on it,
Directing the traffic into pandemonium,
Bowing to bystander cheers.

Police would take him away,
Feed him, pass the time, let him go.
Korky Strumpledon – the city character,
Walked out on his family.
Had no choice, this was a long time ago.

His two boys watched cartoons,
His wife, Thelma, prepared the tea,
And asked Korky to go get some milk.
He was out of work, so did many chores,
With doleful acceptability.

Needless to say, he never went back,
He had already lost them, that, he knew.
Shortly afterwards whilst working backstage
For food, in a rundown theatre,
He lost his mind, or rather, it slipped askew.

Donning his present garb, from a basket
Of cast offs, he went on to find his role.
For a couple of years now, he's gained recognition,
"Hey, Korky, how ya doin'?"
King Korky of street life, takin' his stroll…

Korky was served the best meal of his life.
He unwinds in a chair, that has a woman's embrace.
The man opposite wants to know all about him,
So Korky spills all and the audience laughs…
Korky Strumpledon, has become a TV face.

Just as he did, when he went for the milk,
Once again, Korky never looked back.
He now hosts his own show,
Shares a house with contentment…
And his life is back on track.

I Have Your Eyes

I have your eyes within my heart
I have your heart within my eyes
Feeling what you see,
Seeing lows and highs.

I have your hand within my hand
Walking 'neath English skies
And in my mind I always hear
Those sultry, purple, needy sighs.

I have your wisdom by my side
And our God is everywhere.
Walking meadows alone with you,
An answer to a prayer.
I take you to the highest hill
That overlooks the sea
And hug you warm,
Against the wind...
And stand alone reflectively.

The wind grows teeth
Burrowing underneath clothes,
Chomping, tearing at flesh.
Far below, it whips up sea spray.
A fishing trawler laden with a night's harvest
Bucks and dives towards home.

High above
A lone gull effortlessly wind surfs.

Close by, a paper cup
Traces irregular arcs across the grass,
Coming to rest between my feet.
It has a white seam, a white lip.
For the most part it is royal blue,
With golden print, reading
'I'm nuts for you'.

The wind plays pan pipes on the cup,
The gull soars and gladly cries,
The trawler's home and ropes are thrown
And I have your heart
And I have your eyes.

Hotel Desolate

The reflection of a beautiful woman
Bounces back to me from the still pond,
My thoughts take a stroll backwards
Down dark allies and lonely lanes,
My eyes pierce forward to the strange beyond.

The reflection of a very proud man
Bounces back to me from the still pond,
I leave my body to see my tears.
I fall to my knees amidst this deep magic,
And there is no fairy to wave her wand.

Reflections back to back, silhouettes.
Silent, still memories held in a photo frame.
Like a forsaken, desolate hotel
My mind is home to silent guests.
The candle of life supports a dying flame.

Blindness

I understand
I cannot see,
From noise and worry
I always flee.
Visions unfolding
Mind beholding,
This back-breaking burden
Is crushing me.
Shadows surround
Enclosing sounds
Time goes by
In leaps and bounds.
Colours contracting,
My mind's acting
And visions are dancing around.
Then…..in the distance
I hear a bird…..

How hard it is to picture a sound.

ST. MILDREDS
HALL

Live From St. Mildred's Hall

(Action)

I am Jane Edwards.

(Camera zooms close to capture famous eyes)

I'm reporting from St. Mildred's Hall,
Under a bright sky and a climbing, searing sun.

Such a beautiful setting, I think you'll agree.
From the front of this 16th century house,
Such a large expanse of manicured lawns.

(Camera pans wide)

High-rise, majestically graceful sprinklers
Swing to and forth whilst slightly bowing
In acknowledgement to the beauty they enhance.
The lawns sweep down in layers as far as Dobb's Lane.
The lane encircles the village of St. Mildred's.
Until 18 years ago, the house was a working farmhouse.
With the decline of the farming industry,
St. Mildred's Hall closed down, as did so many others.
But now, even a cursory glance…

(Camera to the house)

Enlightens one to the fact that the house
And grounds are lived, loved and lavished.

(Camera pans down Jane to ground level)

As you can see, I have someone with me.
His name is Mister Chargrill, a Great Dane.
He is the lord and master of all he surveys…

(Camera zooms to Mr Chargrill licking Jane's hand)

And Mister Chargrill says a big thank you
To all supporters of St. Mildred's Dog Rescue.

St Mildred's Hall is a home for rescued dogs.
Mr Chargrill is a permanent occupant.

(Cut to the back of St. Mildred's Hall – pan the kennels)

Here, at the rear of the hall………
I hope you can hear me above the racket of the residents,
One can see the purpose of this establishment.
We have here 92 heated air-con kennels with runs.
Every one of the residents are taken on daily
Freedom runs in the grounds,
By a cross-section of voluntary staff.
The dogs are, in time, given to
Responsible owners, in return for donations.
As you can see…

(Camera follows Jane and dog as she walks)

As I walk down the corridors of kennels,
The very presence of Mister Chargrill,
Quietens the energised canines.

This programme is all about Mister Chargrill,
And what we are about to reveal will astound you.
See you in a couple of minutes.

(Cut to advertisements)

(Camera on Jane sitting on bench with dog at her feet)

Mister C. wasn't cruelly treated prior to St. Mildred's.
At three months he joined Mr. & Mrs. Southwold,
A retired couple.
They lived in an isolated house in St. Mildred's,
And he became the child they couldn't have.
One year later, Mr. Southwold died suddenly,
A brain tumour,
Leaving Mrs. Southwold to deal with her grief,
And to dote on Mr. C, like a true son.
Mr. C. and Mrs. Southwold were family companions
For three long and loving years.
And then, alone in the house with Mr. Chargrill,
Mrs. Southwold was taken seriously ill
With a stroke.
Mister Chargrill was alone.

(Camera sweeps to Jane's hand patting dog's head)

Mrs. Southwold lay paralysed on her bed.

(Close up of Jane's tear-filled famous eyes)

Mister Chargrill spent many days by her side.
Senses on alert, knowing bad was going down.
He grabbed a hand towel from a bedroom stool,
In his jaws,
Dragged it downstairs to the hall
And into his bowl of water.
Then he returned to the bedroom, on to the bed
And draped it slowly over Mrs. Southwold's mouth.
And he repeated this over and over.
This kept her alive.

(Camera roves around kennels as Jane reports)

Two weeks later, they found Mister Chargrill,
Lying beside Mrs. Southwold.

(Quick camera shot of Jane's face – back to kennels)

Mrs. Southwold never fully recovered,
She now resides in Violet Shades Nursing Home.

So… back to St. Mildred's Dog Rescue…

*(Wide shot, sitting on a bench with dog in front of house,
Lawn sprinklers as background)*

St. Mildred's Dog Rescue was founded by Jemma Bywater.
Suffice it to say, she is an animal hypnotherapist,
Who had initial funding from the RSPCA,
On the basis of her remarkable history.

The RSPCA treated Mister Chargrill initially.
After four weeks he was up and around,
Eating drinking and fitfully sleeping,
Mentally, he was profoundly unwell,
So he was placed in the loving care of Jemma.

*(Camera zooms into dog's face as he chuffs twice, blowing
out his jowls, laughing)*

After six months of TLC,
Mr. C. began to demonstrate some 'peculiarities.'

More sadness but with happier endings.
Jemma was treated for
A broken wrist, after falling off her bike.
A few hours after treatment,
She sat on this very bench,
Her wrist was plastered and painful…………
Until Mister Chargrill sat at her feet
And the pain vanished.
Not gradually, no flashing lights,
No visions of Jesus,
No stroking Mister Chargrill…
The pain just up and went.
Later, an x-ray showed no sign of broken bone,
Not even an old fracture.

Later tonight, Jemma will be telling her own story.

In Jemma's words she 'connected with Mr. C. that day'.
And Mister Chargrill has since shone.
Dogs are brought in emaciated, wasted, injured,
Cruelly treated and so very demented, often sad.

All Mr. C. does is walk by,
Giving a sideways glance.
They perk immediately…
Broken bones are mended,
Wagging tails replace dejection,
Wounds rapidly heal.

Mister Chargrill chuffs once as he passes,
He laughs, he smiles and wags his tail.
All of this is verified by Jemma
In our later interview.
In the meantime, let me shake Mr. C's paw.

(Camera frames hand and mutt's paw)

And to this day
Mister Chargrill remains an astute,
Remarkable, enigmatic dog.

Please tune into Jemma's interview,
In thirty minutes and
Hear first-hand
About her life and experiences
With our remarkable Mister Chargrill.

(Camera closes on the dog – fades – goes to ads)

Violet Shades

A pocket full of years ago
I moved into
Violet Shades Rest Home.
I like it here
But I don't like the company
Because I've lost some of my mind
You see.

I am aware of this,
And sometimes
My thoughts take a stroll
Or stride a strut
Eventually rolling into
A sticky, muddy rut.

Once, I had a life,
I was a wife,
But he's long gone,
Deader than a Pharoe's finger nail.
Had three daughters
Got two now.

Mary who was childless
Was a victim
Of drunken driving,
She was the driver.
Jennifer had two kids,
Alice had three.

So that's five grandkids for me.
Think I've seen two of 'em,
Don't know what they were,
But it's good enough,
It'll do.

Like in the War
Jack went abroad.
I've never been abroad,
I like it here,
Nothing to fear,
Only the way others tend to leave.

Food's good, nothing to chew
He got shot in Italy
He told me in a letter
But I already knew.

Every bagful of days
They do my hair
There's none on top, plenty on the sides
And back.
A look in the mirror
Makes me laugh
Then I get wet,
It doesn't smell
Perhaps I can't tell
What the hell.

Sleep comes easy here
Trouble is
Not at night-time.

The noise of them aeroplanes
Made me nervous
And they were our planes.

I used to knit in here
But now my fingers are bent
Can't remember
Where the straightness went.

I think one grandkid was
A boy called Rod,
Named after a singer
Poor sod.
Perhaps without my cataracts
I wouldn't like this place so much.

I'd like to see the Sun.
Curtains always closed
To watch TV.
Trouble is nobody watches
They're always asleep
Or staring into space
With drool on their faces.

Don't feel so good today
Left my teeth in my bedroom
Could be a bonus,
Can grin and show my gums
To the nurse of doom
When she wheels in the pills.

Must go now, Jack,
This is only a mind letter,
I'll get somebody to write it.
It might read a lot better.

Dicky-Bubby

Poor little dicky-bubby lying on the ground
Used to be so pretty when flying all around.
Pretty little dicky-bubby sitting on the fence
Darting into bushes, prickly and so dense.

Cute little dicky-bubby tweeting all day long,
All the other dicky-bubbies listening to his song.
Playful little dicky-bubby tugging at a worm
Stretching it and pulling it and forcing it to squirm.

Tired little dicky-bubby bathing in the Sun
Slumbering and snoozing until the day is done.
Brave little dicky-bubby soaring in the breeze
Diving from on high to his home in the trees.

Now his home's in Heaven flying high with Mum and Dad,
And the dicky-bubbies left behind are very, very sad.
Poor little dicky-bubby lying on the ground
Used to be so pretty when flying all around.

Jurassic Swinger

Now, at last, I am wiser,
I have seen most things, done most things
I am nobody's fool, perhaps I am cool,
But I am definitely drastically older!
I cannot run, it's a pain to walk,
I put my brain in gear, before I can talk.
Hey! Mr. Sadness! Get off my shoulder!

Paint me green, I'll be a black soul singer,
Paint me pink, I will free China,
I'm painted white; so that's my plight,
And I am definitely drastically older!
I don't find it hard to stay in bed,
Constantly thinking what it's like to be dead.
Hey! Mr. Sadness! Get off my shoulder!

At last I've got my hair to look right
I can be polite and non-sexist.
I can handle romance, and kid…can I dance!
But I am definitely drastically older!
My face which was smooth, now covered in grooves
And nothing important ever moves!
Hey! Mr. Sadness! Get off my shoulder!

Come on, Mr. Sadness, leave me alone
My life is my own, let me live it.
If I want to sit down or jive and get down
Then it's down to you to just give it.
You know, Mr. Sadness, I hate goodbyes
But it's time you found another shoulder.
So tell the truth, I don't like your lies,
And I know I'm getting older!

Layers

If only I could tell you his name,
Nationality
His whereabouts
A clue to identity
Fragment of history.

His devious ruses,
Irrationality,
Subtle brutality,
Tension-filled mind games.
Oh, to show you the bruises.

………………..

He invited me into his life.
He took me in.
Said I didn't have a life.
He was right
Yet he still took me in.

I couldn't have loved him more.
But from that first night
The layers gradually peeled,
Over several arduous years
And gallons of tears.

I dressed for every occasion,
Breakfast, when he came home.
When his friends visited
For men games.
Always dressed to order.

To cross a border
Meant punishment of the highest order,
Though often subtle.
Dressed for supper, dressed for bed.
Always dressed with attitude.

Not regular meals
But timed to instruction,
Never early or late.
Laundry cleaned, pressed,
But never to be seen in action.

Any infraction
Was duly dealt with.

And I kept peeling layers
Hoping for ground zero,
To love him more
For what he was and what he wasn't…
But there was no 'wasn't'.

Not once did he take me out.
I went alone, shopping.
He always found out
If I stopped for a coffee and chat…
He never broke a bone in my body.

I kept the results secret.
At twelve weeks I told him,
Hoping for happiness to break through.
We'd never talked about family.
Fists pounded 'til my belly was blue.

He left after that,
Said I was soiled.
Later, when found drowning in misery,
I was taken to my room
In a home for the lost and madly insane.

He still has my number,
Visits twice a year.
Says he's my Father.
He's not my Father.
He squeezes my mind in a vice of fear.

If I gave you a clue
As to who he is,
He has bombs planted in this home.
And may I assure you, he would know.
He's a gentleman on the surface.

When my time comes
To feed the ground,
Then, hopefully, these words will be found.
To warn others to peel layers to the core.

I will lie restless always
Beneath God's Earth
With my baby.
I never gave birth.

When his time comes
His layers will be left behind.
He will be judged for what he is –
A soulless, sinister, evil mind.

Raw Nature

The Sun bleeds crimson
Over a vast Savannah.
I stop to urinate,
Then I and my invisible friend
Walk hand in hand
Into oblivion.

Universe Queen

Why did you ever leave me?
You went without a care.
You hurt me but I'll remember
The love that lingered there.
I'm lonely,
But I find comfort,
When I argue with myself,
When I wonder at the stars
That rest upon God's shelf.
You've left me broken-hearted
But I'll be alright soon.
But when my heart is mended
Man's home will be the Moon.
Why is it your love should wither
Upon a day I noticed it most?
One second we're close together
And then you're gone just like a ghost.
Oh, darling, I know
We'll never meet again,
So let me tell you this,
That all this heartache, grief and pain
Will never overcome the bliss
Of those few months of happiness,
With never a moment blue,
When you could have been… My Universe Queen
And I would always love you.

Jazz 'n' Chief

Chief wore a filthy straggly wig
Under a torn and stained woollen hat.
His grubby face filled with sores
Was lined, ancient, somehow wise.

Sporting a crumpled lumberjack shirt
Under a hooded coat, minus the hood.
Soiled grimy trousers, too short,
Hands in his pockets, oh, and no flies.

His feet were filthy and bare
Under red, plastic, open sandals.
In one hand he carried a hold-all.
He sat on a bar stool, bag on the floor.

Jazz was a man dressed as a woman,
Served at The Street Den for years.
He/she greeted Chief with a wink and
Been some time, and began to pour.

Chief's drink was malt, glass 'n' bottle,
Nice to be back, pour yerself one, Jazz
He/she did just that and blew him a kiss,
To the wails of Stevie W, 'I Just Called'.

Place was empty 'cept for Jazz and Chief.
No windows to the street, no distractions.
Place smelled of chuck-ups, toilets, smoke,
Gimme yer hand, Chief drawled.

Jazz's arm appeared like a swan's neck,
Chief held the limp hand gracefully offered.
Yer know, Jazz, ah bin 'avin' troubles of late
As Jazz whispered in his ear, his wig danced.

They shared a bottle, and Chief's smile grew
Jazz told him what was a-happenin' 'n' goin' to.
Chief stood, paid from his bag, tipped his old hat,
Then he looked at the door to the street, entranced.

He didn't want to disappear from his secret oasis,
Or cross the threshold to the world beyond.
Armstrong chugged 'Wonderful World'. He cried
Silently, picked up his bag, and stepped to the door.

Stagnant daylight, pollution, traffic, people, chaos
Smacked his senses. He hustled and bustled to the kerb.
A limo crept to a halt by his sandaled feet.
Your carriage awaits, Mr President.
He knows the score.

Lovebird

Refreshed by April showers.
Here we sit upon the Moon,
Watching the world spin by,
I hold my Liz, we kiss and kiss,
Never asking why.
Elizabeth, Elizabeth,
My vision of love come true,
Yes, Princess, this really is
A love I never knew.
Angels sing and honeybees
Buzz, dance and generally tease.
A lovebird on her shoulder,
The Moon, the stars, the tolerant trees.
We walked… and then I told her…
She turned and smiled,
Aching, burning heart…
It was then we knew
We could never part.
Holding hands, we floated high,
I watched our lovebird,
Floating free in ice-blue sky,
Heard its wistful cry.
In love forever...
As the clouds rolled by.

Max B

He likes the bottle and he's full of wind………………
But that's enough about Baby's Dad.
So now here's the real thing:
A poem about Max B to be read,
Today, the day of his Christening.
………………………………………………………..
We often wish for miracles,
And our wishes go unheard,
But Max B is the best kind of miracle,
When we haven't wished a word.
Our lives are ruled by chaos,
As time sprints by so swift.
Then out of the blue springs Baby Max B
And he gave us all a lift. What a gift!!
Being so new, Max B can't do much,
But his face and his eyes say it all.
Feed me, change me, give me a hug,
And watch me trying to crawl!!
In return Max B gives us,
A purity in person, innocence supreme,
A boundless bond for us all to share,
And a future for us to dream.
Max B is but one in 7.3 billion,
An early delivery to Ma and Pa.
Yet Max now shines so brightly…
Twinkle, twinkle,
Twinkle on, you little star.

Kahlia B

Look closely at the morning dew,
Diamond-dusted, delicate lace,
Full of promise for the forthcoming day,
Just like the eyes of Kahlia Grace.

She arrived as a tiny parcel,
Perfect in every way,
Except, that is, for her gangster's glare,
Which was there on the very first day.
Don't mess with me, says the sullen stare,
A gift from her Dad, no doubt.
But her smile makes up for this serious scowl,
When her face is sunshine throughout.

All's worthwhile when Kahlia smiles,
She's made a house a home.
Mum and Dad are now a family,
Wherever they may roam.
There's a bond between Kahlia and Mum,
In many ways, that comes across.
A closeness beyond description,
With Kahlia Grace the boss.

There's a bond between Kahlia and Dad,
He's protective in many ways.
But when Kahlia can talk instead of squawk,
He will always do what she says.
The brightest star in the sky,
Fell silently to Earth,
On the night Kahlia's Mum gave birth.

Kahlia, a precious baby girl.
Welcome, Kahlia, to our world.